I0078294

Praise for *unprideful light*

Chontali's book on timidity speaks to every person who struggles with obeying God's call on their lives. It's not just about shrinking back and being shy; its more about our own pride of what we think God can't do. After reading this book and working through the reflection questions, readers will find themselves pursuing God's call and going where He is sending them, even if they feel ill equipped at that moment. Our prayer for you, the reader, is that you will come across your own encounter with God in those moments of doubt, and that when you hear Him say, "Whom shall I send?" your response will be, "Here I am, Lord; send me."
 — PASTOR PETER AND DR. DIDI WATTS
   The Rock Church, Los Angeles

I really enjoyed Chontali's book. It caused me to think of timidity in a different way and see how it stops God from moving in our lives. The questions at the end of the chapters were engaging and caused me to do some deep self-reflection about moments of timidity in my life. This book is a must-read if you are struggling with stepping out of your comfort zone and wanting to walk in your purpose!
 — TORISHA MONDAY, *Certified Life Coach*

Chontali has been given a REMARKABLE gift from the One True God. She has unpacked the concepts of timidity and fear using historical biblical figures. She has beautifully showcased how God's power deflects fear and timidity and renames the person who obeys. The structure of her work gives us a deep depiction of Elijah and Gideon, just to name a few, and how God takes AMAZING care of His people. If you've not read this piece of literature, I encourage you to. It will lead you to a deeper understanding and love of the Lord Jesus Christ, our Redeemer, our Savior, our Friend. In the words of Chontali, God remains committed, despite our timidity and fear.

— CHRISTINE MANER, *Counselor / Educator*

Unprideful Light *is a wonderful resource for everyone struggling with timidity and false humility. This book personally ministered to me about the tendency to hold back due to the illusion and feelings of inadequacy fed by the enemy of our souls. Chontali does an exceptional job of connecting the lives of biblical people like Moses to modern day people in the 21st century. The principles in this book are life changing and thought provoking.*

— MARIA ROBINSON, *Author / Ministry Leader*

Chontali wonderfully unpacks biblical stories of the pridefully timid, who have been using their timidity to not walk fully in God's calling. In each story, Chontali highlights that when God calls a person, He also provides the strength to move with Him. She reminds us that it is through our weakness, where we find God, and that it is our God who will strengthen us into the warriors that we are in Him. Having gone through many seasons of deafness, timidity, and questioning God, I am reminded that being too timid to step out in faith, especially when He has called me, is in fact a betrayal to the God who loves me so deeply. This book will call out the sinful nature within us, but will also gently pull us in to the abundance and power of the great I Am.

— ROBIN YI, *Educator*

I've known Chontali since we were in elementary school together, and she has always possessed a wise spirit. This book is just an extension of the woman of God she has become. Chontali beautifully illustrates the connection between biblical stories and present life application. The reader can relate, soak up the encouragement she has spelled out on the pages of this book, and be challenged by the guiding questions she offers to deepen your relationship with the Lord.

— JENNIFER J. JONES, LMFT 97584

unprideful light:
winning the battle against timidity

chontali kirk

kirk media llc
Los Angeles, CA

unprideful light:
winning the battle against timidity
chontali herod-kirk

No part of this book may be reproduced or
transmitted in any form or by any means, electronic
or mechanical, including photocopying, recording, or
by any information storage and retrieval system,
without permission in writing from the publisher.

For Spiritual and Informational Purposes Only.
The information provided in this book is for spiritual
and informational purposes only, and solely as a
self-help tool for your own use. This book is not a
replacement for therapy, counseling, or medical
advice.

THE HOLY BIBLE, NEW INTERNATIONAL
VERSION®, NIV® Copyright © 1973, 1978, 1984,
2011 by Biblica, Inc.™ Used by permission. All
rights reserved worldwide.

ISBN 978-1-7355108-1-1

The Publishing Team:
Kirk Media LLC
Edited by Emily Slason

Printed in the United States of America
© 2020 Chontali Herod-Kirk. All rights reserved.

First Printing
1 2 3 4 5 6 8 9 10

This book is dedicated to all who need to be reminded of how damaging it is to shrink back.

Also, to my Spiritual Giants:
Robert Kirk
Taylor Kirk
Delissa Jeffries-Herod
George Herod
Rhoen Moore
Janetta Maxwell
Apostle Jacque Harris
Georgia Flowers (Rest in power)
Lillian Jeffries (Rest in power)
Dr. Donald Ferguson
Mother Marilyn Ferguson (Rest in power)
~ I love you ~

Join the *Unprideful Light* Community:

www.chontalikirk.com

How To Use This Book

At the end of each chapter are questions to respond to in an individual or group setting. These questions are designed to help you apply Biblical principles to your life and courageously overcome fear and timidity. I pray for life-changing experiences!

contents

foreword

WHEN I READ Chontali's *Unprideful Light*, the first word that came to me was *transformational*. Immediately, I was challenged to do a self-check for any pride (timidity) that may have been in me and potentially blocking what God wanted to do in my life. This is the sign of an excellent book — one that grabs you and impacts you personally. I was unable to put it down once I got started.

Like so many, I was used to thinking of pride from the perspective of one who has an unhealthy sense of self, erected before others and before God. The kind of pride that keeps people from asking for help, because of fear of diminishing an image or reputation. The kind of pride that exalts itself over the will of God. I hadn't viewed timidity as an issue of pride. But, in the *Unprideful Light*, Chontali uses characters of the Bible to illustrate how timidity shows up in the life of those called by God to do something great.

I was called into ministry at age twenty-four. It was evident early on that the anointing on my life was in the area of preaching. However, if I could have made legitimate excuses to get out of every single preaching opportunity, I would have done just that, because for at least the first ten years of ministry, I never felt fully worthy of the calling on my life, nor the opportunities God had given me. And it's important to acknowledge that being good at something does not automatically mean one is not timid.

It took me years to overcome the pride of timidity. I would always ask God, "Why me? Who, me? Isn't there anyone else but me?" This was a serious challenge for me. On the outside, I appeared confident and sure; but on the inside, I questioned every step I took. What finally broke the timidity was a clear understanding that God made no mistakes in whom He chooses. I was blessed to receive positive mentoring and encouragement from truly God-sent men and women. I had to learn that my timidity worked in conflict to God's call on my life. Timidity made doing the assignment more difficult. The internal battle that raged in me made it hard to bask in the blessing. In hindsight, having a book like *Unprideful Light*, would have been the miracle message I desperately needed at that time.

To anyone emerging in your purpose, and especially to those answering the call to do ministry, this *is* the book to read. Even if you feel as though the pride of timidity is not your leading issue, this book will be helpful in assisting you to "examine self" to ensure you are not blocking the work that God wants to do in you.

Young Timothy of the New Testament struggled with timidity, which is why Paul had to instruct him not to allow anyone to question his call or the value of his teaching and preaching. Paul calls it out directly and says, "Fan the Flame," and know that the Lord had not given us the spirit of fear (timidity) but of power, love and a sound mind *(2 Timothy 1:6-7).*

As you read *Unprideful Light*, my hope is you'll be compelled to search for any pride of timidity in you; question how it might be hindering you from executing God's plan for your life, and thoroughly turn that thing over to the Lord, who is the Author and Finisher of our faith. I am so grateful the Lord met me at my seasons of timidity and enabled me to overcome them, so I could fully answer the call on my life. I only wish

I had this book early in my ministry to help me navigate my challenges, sooner rather than later. For all the times I questioned my preaching, *Unprideful Light* really could have been a great help in lifting some of the burdens I had placed on myself. So, it is with confidence that I say, this book should be required reading, especially for emerging leaders of the 21st Century Church.

You will get a lot out of this simple, yet poignant book. In *Unprideful Light,* Chontali does the topic of timidity justice, and makes a timely application that will bless anyone who reads it.

Blessings!
Dr. Najuma Smith-Pollard
Pastor, Word of Encouragement Church

note

L IFE HAS A WAY of silencing the voices that have the power to speak to the most inner parts of who we are. Loss, rejection, circumstances, and unfortunate events will rob us of the opportunity to speak truth to power. Without the ability to recognize these opportunities, we could forever be in the abyss of not trusting who we were truly created to be. *Unprideful Light* is a perfect depiction of how Chontali made the life-altering decision to choose to not allow her gift to be buried under the lies that life has more power than she does. Her commitment to overcome timidity is one many people don't know is possible until they see that someone else has had victory in that arena. Walking with her through a season of her journey truly brings this book to life. The methods outlined in the book are not just the theoretical suggestions formed from research, but the real-life tools she used to overcome. There are no lofty, unrealistic promises, but the graceful work she underwent to deliver a project that helps unlock the freedom so many desperately need. This book is not only revelation knowledge, but it is life-giving power to those trapped behind the trick of timidity. Walk into His marvelous light to join Chontali on the path to boldness and faith in what God says about you.

Chante Truscott
Founder, Wives in Waiting

introduction

BY DEFINITION, pride means *inordinate* or *excessive self-esteem*. Most would focus on pride as having excessively *high* self-esteem, but this definition leaves room for pride to also mean having excessively **low** self-esteem. For the purpose of this book, we will define pride as "choosing to believe one's own thoughts and follow one's own will over God's thoughts and God's will."

Psalm 10:4 states: *"In his pride, the wicked man does not seek him; in all his thoughts, there is no room for God."* When we allow our minds to be so filled with our own thoughts, and when we neglect to seek God to fill our minds with His word, then the result is pride. Choosing to believe our own thoughts over God's thoughts is pride, and if we're honest, all of us have struggled in this area. This book focuses on the pride that comes from *timidity,* or lack of courage and confidence.

I have struggled with pride for most of my life. Not the pride that looks like someone bragging about their competence or importance — but the pride that believes *I am not good enough.* Often, I would feel worthless and unable to be used for God's glory. These thoughts would exalt above God's thoughts and plans for my life. I would feel ensnared in timidity, self-pity, depression, and anxiety. I thought I was too awkward to converse with others and influence them in any way.

As Christians, we are supposed to believe that these negative thoughts are all lies. The Bible says to cast down every imagination that exalts itself against the knowledge of God (1 Corinthians 10:5). The knowledge of God is that we are fearfully and wonderfully made (Psalm 139:14). We are God's treasure and a peculiar people (1 Peter 2:9). We are the light of the world that shall not be hidden underneath a bowl (Matthew 5:14-16). All of these things are good and true (Philippians 4:8).

But, if we're honest, at times we still may believe in the lie that we aren't good enough. Sometimes we feel insecure, and this insecurity can prevent us from obeying the Lord. *How so?* you might ask. This is how: timidity can cripple us and hinder us from doing what God wants us to do. At this point, timidity is not *just* harmful. It's not *just* intimidation. It becomes an excuse to disobey God. This book is to show you examples of when people of God battled with timidity — when they were slow to move because they were too afraid, or felt like they weren't good enough.

With this book, it is my hope that you will gather strength in God's word and use it to gain control of the timidity in your life. May you use the strength from God's word to transform into His **unprideful light.**

-*Chontali*

Philippians 4:4-7
"Rejoice in the LORD always. I will say it again: Rejoice! Let your gentleness be evident to all. The LORD is near. Do not be anxious about anything, but in every situation, by prayer and petition, with thanksgiving, present your requests to God. And the peace of God, which transcends all understanding, will guard your hearts and your minds in Christ Jesus. Finally, brothers and sisters, whatever is true, whatever is noble, whatever is right, whatever is pure, whatever is lovely, whatever is admirable — if anything is excellent or praiseworthy — think about such things. Whatever you have learned or received or heard from me, or seen in me — ***put it into practice.***

And the peace of GOD, which transcends all understanding, will guard your hearts and your minds in Christ Jesus."

Romans 12:2
"Do not conform to the pattern of this world, but be transformed by the renewing of your mind. Then you will be able to test and approve what God's will is — His good, pleasing and perfect will."

one
what happened to moses?

EXODUS 1-3 TEACHES us about a Hebrew child who was spared from an Egyptian pharaoh's death sentence to all Hebrew infant boys. This child was saved by two midwives, his mother, his sister, and an Egyptian princess, who would later become his adoptive mother. Because of these women, this Hebrew child was raised and educated in an Egyptian palace, learned how to speak well, and act powerfully (Acts 7:22). This child grew up to be the man we know as Moses, the one who would deliver God's people from slavery.

If you ask me, a person with this type of upbringing seems like the perfect candidate to lead God's people out of bondage. Moses seemed to have good character and balance; he was aware that he was the son of enslaved Hebrews, even though he had the privilege of the royal Egyptians. Moses had both perspectives: he was a Hebrew who knew the lifestyle of the Egyptians. He could have been the perfect leader to bridge the gap between the two cultures.

So, what changed about Moses? Why is it that when God called Moses to lead His people out of slavery, Moses replied that he was weak and unqualified (Exodus 3:11)? We know that Moses was trained by the best of the royal class and learned how to speak well (Acts 7:22), so what caused his confidence to drop so low that he claimed to have *never* been eloquent (Exodus 4:10)? Why did Moses feel so incapable of leading God's people to freedom, that he asked God to choose another person

(Exodus 4:13)? *What happened to Moses?*

According to the Bible, it was one day of brave yet impulsive actions that affected Moses—the day he went outside the palace walls and defended an enslaved Hebrew person. This experience changed his life forever and triggered the unraveling of his confidence. But, this day also set Moses on the course to becoming the liberator of God's people.

When a forty-year-old Moses went out to check on his enslaved relatives, his purpose was ignited. On this day, Moses saw how his people were being abused. When he witnessed an Egyptian striking an enslaved Hebrew, he murdered the Egyptian. When word got to the pharaoh that Moses had killed the Egyptian to save the enslaved Hebrew, the pharaoh sought to kill Moses. This pushed Moses to run away from Egypt to Midian in exile.

Moses spent forty years in Midian, living a *hidden life under the radar*. He married and had children. Being a husband and father did not cancel the purpose God had for his life. There was evidence of Moses' reflection in the way that he named his children, mainly Gershom, whose name means *sojourner,* or a temporary stay in a foreign land. After forty years in Midian, Moses' *hidden* life was interrupted by a bush with God's voice speaking

MOSES' DIM AND GRIM CIRCUMSTANCES WERE ABOUT TO BE BRIGHTENED **BY THE LIGHT OF THE WORLD,** WHO WOULD CALL HIM ONCE AGAIN TO SAVE THE ENSLAVED HEBREWS.

from it. This bush, which was on Mount Horeb, or also known as the mountain of God, was bright and in flames, but it was not consumed by the fire. Moses' dim and grim circumstances were about to be brightened by the Light of the world, who would call him once again to save the enslaved Hebrews.

This voice from the burning bush would inform Moses that God was about to deliver His people from the oppression of Egypt, and that He was going to deliver them through Moses (Exodus 3:8, 10). This burning bush was the courage and *unprideful light* — God's light — that Moses needed to succeed in delivering God's people. Despite Moses' numerous excuses and statements of timidity and fear, God remained committed to the decision that He was going to use Moses to deliver His people out of Egypt. God wanted to demonstrate His limitless power for His people. God wanted Moses to focus on His plan, and not on his own limited abilities.

> GOD WANTED MOSES TO FOCUS ON HIS PLAN, AND NOT ON HIS OWN LIMITED ABILITIES.

Does this story sound like yours? Growing up, did you think life would be purposeful, but now it feels mundane and unfulfilling? Do you ever find yourself asking *what happened* to your life? Do you wonder how you wound up in such a place?

Like Moses, you may have felt more secure in your youth, but then a traumatic event occurred that left you doubting yourself and your life's purpose. Sometimes, life hands us events that leave us feeling like we don't measure up. Even when an opportunity presents itself, we may feel that someone else can do the job better, and we choose to not pursue it.

The Bible says that we overcome by the blood of the Lamb and by the word of our testimony (Revelations 12:11). Therefore, if Moses' story sounds like yours, then you don't have to revel in it or remain in doubt. You can overcome your timidity and fears by remembering Moses' story. Even truer, you can overcome your timidity and fears by knowing **God's strength** through Moses' weakness. The same God that called Moses and gave him His strength to deliver thousands of enslaved people from Egypt to the promised land of freedom, is the same God who has called you and me to do great things for His glory. Like Moses, our lives are less about us, and more about God saving His people from sin, bondage, and captivity. Our lives are more about God's goal of showing His people the love and freedom they can experience through Christ. We all have a part to play in God's goal. There is one Man, our Maker, who has called us to help reach this goal, and He never lifts the call. Our excuses and insecurities cannot lift the call. We are marked for life. His word is true and it stands through all the stages of our lives.

Your call does not disappear because of a traumatic event. What does disappear is time. We have a certain amount of time in our lives. God can redeem time if we start late in living His will, *but* nevertheless, there is a time limit, so it is very important that we trust God with our lives and know that He will perform His works through us, if we avail ourselves. He can do great things when we allow Him to shine His light and power through us. When you trust God and you build yourself up in scripture, your faith grows. You are building yourself and your experiences so that you can share testimonies to help others. Looking back, you may realize how much time has passed that you have lived in dormancy and defeat. God knows how to make that time count for more than just being *wasted*. God is a redeemer of time. He can use everything thing you've gone through for good the moment you decide to walk in your calling.

Here's proof: when God called Moses in Midian, he found Moses shepherding sheep. Little did Moses know, he would soon be shepherding God's people out of Egypt. God is a Master Architect; he can move all the parts of your life—the exciting, the traumatic, and the mundane— so *all* of it aligns to His will.

> HIS PROMISES ARE NOT CONDITIONAL TO OUR ABILITIES, BUT ARE INSTEAD CONDITIONAL TO OUR OBEDIENCE.

So, I encourage you to consider Moses as a man who had a tragic experience, like many of us have had, and had to relearn who it was God made him to be. Many of us have to relearn the truths of His word and the truths of His promises for our lives. May we be enlightened in the fact that His promises are not conditional to our abilities, but are instead conditional to our obedience. We may not have a burning bush to talk to like Moses did, but we do have God's word to follow and obey. May we walk in God's obedience and fearlessly carry the light of His word in us. God can use us in any stage of life.

Meditation Scriptures:

Psalm 119:105- *Your word is a lamp for my feet, and a light on my path.*

Psalm 119:11- *I have treasured Your word in my heart so that I may not sin against You.*

Hebrews 4:12-13- *For the word of God is living and effective and sharper than any double-edged sword, penetrating as far as the separation of soul and spirit, joints, and marrow. It is able to judge the thoughts and intentions of the heart. No creature is hidden from Him, but all things are naked and exposed to the eyes of Him to whom we must give an account.*

Burning Bush Moment:

1. When you were younger, what did you feel was your life's purpose?

2. What crisis happened to make you doubt that you could fulfill this purpose?

3. What are you committed to now?

4. How can your current commitments help you fulfill the purpose that was revealed to you when you were younger?

5. How do your current commitments relate to the purpose revealed to you in your childhood?

two
gideon's new
identity

YEARS AFTER GOD used Moses to lead His people out of slavery and into their promised land, the people of God were settled comfortably in their new life. In fact, they became so comfortable that they forgot to tell their children about God and how He had saved them. Generation after generation passed, and people learned less and less about their God because their parents failed to teach them. While they were forgetting about their God and all He had done for them and could do for them, they were turning to false gods like Asherah and Baal — gods of fertility they believed would bless their land and make their crops grow. The problem with this was these gods weren't doing anything to solve the poverty that the Israelites were now experiencing. Still, they refused to turn away from their fruitless, false gods.

As a result, the Midianites and other enemy camps were able to terrorize the Israelites. They looted their land and crops because God's people had rejected Him to worship other gods, and this caused them to forfeit God's covering and protection over them (Judges 6:10). The terror was so strong that many of them lived in hiding, retreating in caves and dens (Judges 6:2). The Hebrews were vulnerable once again, and they cried out to God for help. God heard them, and He raised up a leader to rescue them.

The leader whom God chose was found hiding. This soon-to-be leader was so afraid the enemy camps would try to hurt him or steal from him, that he was found threshing wheat in a winepress instead of a threshing floor. The winepress was a large hole that was dug into the earth and meant for pressing grapes. The threshing floor was a large stone above ground meant for threshing wheat and gathering the grains that fell after the chaff was blown away by the method of wind winnowing. Now just imagine for a second, how likely it was for the wind to blow away the chaff in a winepress. I'd say it was highly unlikely. But, Gideon cautiously and fearfully threshed wheat in a winepress. Then, an angel of God appeared to him.

When the angel of God appeared to Gideon — this timid man — something unexpected happened. The angel of God's first words to Gideon were "The Lord is with you, **mighty warrior**." About whom was God talking? Surely, not this man who was hiding, plagued and paralyzed by fear! Gideon seemed just as dumbfounded as we are. How could he be a mighty warrior if his land was being overtaken and his people were being terrorized by enemy camps? How could he be a mighty warrior if his family was of low status? Above all, how could he be called a mighty warrior if he himself held the lowest ranking within his already low-ranked family?

As far as God was concerned, Gideon's only problem was one of hearing. Gideon had no problems hearing the many insecure thoughts that ran rampant in his head. What he *did* have a problem hearing, was God saying *why* he was a mighty warrior. God called Gideon a mighty warrior because *the Lord was with him*, and through Gideon, God would overcome the enemy camps who oppressed His people.

> GOD CALLED GIDEON A MIGHTY WARRIOR **BECAUSE THE LORD WAS WITH HIM**, AND THROUGH GIDEON, GOD WOULD OVERCOME THE ENEMY CAMPS WHO OPPRESSED HIS PEOPLE.

What happened next? We know that God called Gideon to save the Israelites from those who taunted them. But before we even get into how Gideon led an army to save God's people, let's bring attention to how Gideon's name — which relates to his identity — changed immediately after he obeyed God.

We know that Gideon's first task was to destroy his family's idol statues, and build an altar for God in their place. This was done to honor the true Deliverer of the Israelites, the One who brought them out of Egypt under the leadership of Moses. This act of destroying the idol statues of Baal and others was foreshadowing how Gideon (with God's strength) would eventually save the Israelites, which would take courage. Gideon was so terrified to be caught tearing down these idols that he did it at night; nevertheless, he obeyed God in the midst of his fear (Judges 6:27).

Although Gideon destroyed the idols at night to avoid being caught, people figured out what he did anyway, and they sought to kill him for destroying the statues of their gods. But Gideon's father, Joash, saved his life by raising the idea that if Baal were truly a god, then he could defend himself. The fact that the idol Baal broke so easily made him seem that much more powerless. I'm guessing Joash was successful in convincing the people that Gideon was a **warrior** because he was able to contend with Baal. On that day, the people called Gideon "Jerubbaal," which is Hebrew for *competitor of Baal*, because he was able to tear down Baal's altar. This shows us that when we start to obey God, whether in fear or in boldness, our identity changes. No longer is Gideon looking so timid;

already, he is beginning to look like that **mighty warrior** of which the angel of God spoke. Gideon is becoming someone who is courageous enough to fight for God.

Next, we know that God gave Gideon further instructions, which involved him preparing for a war against the enemy camp that sought to terrorize the Israelites.

We saw a glimpse of the Holy Spirit come upon Gideon, causing him to blow a horn that called many people to rally behind him. Three hundred of these men were eventually called to serve in Gideon's army.

But just because Gideon had obeyed God the first time and was courageous enough to destroy false idols — even gaining a new name because of it — it did not mean that his fears and uncertainties were banished for good.

As if the angel of the Lord appearing to Gideon wasn't enough of a sign that God was with him, we find that Gideon starts to question God, seeking confirmation of his mission to save the Israelites. First, Gideon asked God to perform a miracle by wetting his fleece that was spread on the threshing floor, while keeping the threshing floor dry. God did that. Then, Gideon asked God to wet the ground while keeping the fleece dry. God did that too. Eventually, Gideon had run out of excuses to dodge his mission and he had received enough confirmation to obey God. He formed the army that would lead the Israelites into victory.

In the formation of Gideon's army, God sought to shine so bright as to be the single victor in saving the Israelites. He called for a small army so that no one but He would be able to take the credit. Many men rallied behind Gideon to fight, but God called for a process of elimination. God first called for the elimination of all men who were fearful and trembling. He ordered Gideon to announce that these men may return home (Judges 7:3). The interesting thing about this passage is that this first elimination was a self-elimination. Gideon merely had to announce: *Whoever is trembling with fear, go home,* and 22,000 of the men left. The scriptures don't mention that He ordered people who *looked* scared to go home. I am betting that some of those fighters who remained were indeed fearful and trembling, but they were ready to be courageous and face their fears to gain freedom. Our goal is to prohibit fear from excusing us from fighting for

> WE DON'T ALWAYS GET
> TO SHOW UP CONFIDENT
> AND STRONG.
> BEING WILLING TO FIGHT,
> AFRAID AND ALL,
> IS ENOUGH FOR GOD
> TO BE STRONG IN US.

God. We don't always get to show up confident and strong. Being *willing* to fight, afraid and all, is enough for God to be strong in us.

The second elimination was indeed God sending men home. After the self-elimination, there were still 10,000 people who remained. God didn't want anyone to have a chance to say that they dominated the enemy troops simply with numerical strength. He needed a smaller group. So, God gave them a test to see who could drink water while staying watchful and alert. Those who knelt down to drink were sent home. The three hundred who lapped water with their hands to their mouths were permitted to stay and fight. God wanted this small group of three hundred people to fight the enemy camp they described as "a "swarm of locusts" with camels "as innumerable as the sand on the seashore" (Judges 7:12).

Before the battle, God reassures Gideon once again that his side would win. God told Gideon to spy on the Midianite camp to hear what they had to say about him. Surprisingly, in Judges 7:9-14, one man from the Midianite camp explained to a fellow soldier a dream he had about Gideon's army. The soldier interpreted the dream as a warning that God was indeed with Gideon and that his army would win the battle. After Gideon received insight that the Midianites knew they were likely to lose the battle and that Gideon's army was destined to win, his confidence boosted like never before. The next thing you read is that Gideon's troops (a total of three hundred people) blew horns and followed God's strategy to win the fight against their enemy troops, and they had peace for forty years.

So, what's this about you not having what you need in order to do what you feel God is calling on you to do? What's that you say about how you are not strong enough or qualified enough to work for God? Our God is one who chooses the weak things of the world to shame the strong (1 Corinthians 1:27). His strength is made perfect in our weakness (2 Corinthians 12:9). Too often, we dismiss thoughts and desires that God plants in our minds and in our heart, because we don't feel qualified. We feel inclined to certain callings, but we don't act because we focus on our limited abilities, which are no match to the qualifications of that calling. But, there is a saying that says, *God does not call the qualified; He qualifies whom He calls.* When we work for God's purpose, our abilities don't matter. Only our obedience does. What matters is that we partner with Him and allow Him to work and channel

> WHEN WE WORK FOR GOD'S PURPOSE, OUR ABILITIES DON'T MATTER. ONLY OUR OBEDIENCE DOES.

Himself in us (it's His show, not ours).

Furthermore, when we work for God, we never know what those *better, stronger, and mightier* people are thinking. Many times, people see things in us that we can't fully see for ourselves. There are people who know your potential and power, but they don't want *you* to know your potential and power. They hope you never find out! And then there are others who wish you knew how powerful you are, but you just can't see all the goodness in yourself that they see.

You may not feel mighty, but you will ALWAYS be mighty when you are with your God. I'll state it again: *The people of God will **always** be mighty when they are with their God.* God calls you mighty when you are with Him and when you are courageous enough to obey Him. My hope is that

THE PEOPLE OF GOD WILL ALWAYS BE MIGHTY WHEN THEY ARE WITH THEIR GOD.

you finally learn to identify with the person God has called you to be, even if your current state does not reflect it. Learn to take on God's warrior identity, even if it contradicts how you view yourself or how others view you. Just as Gideon had to overcome his family's idols before he could take back the land for his people, we must overcome the issues from our upbringing that hold us back.

Gideon was called a mighty warrior before he was one. God gave him a new name and helped him grow into that identity. Before he knew it, people recognized that Gideon was bolder and called him *Jerubbaal*, which means one who contends with Baal, as he tore down the statue of Baal for God's namesake. Speak your new name and then grow into it. Crush timidity as if it were a false idol, and make it a habit to courageously obey God in the face of fear.

Courageously obey God and His scriptures by denouncing any lies you believe about yourself, even if they came from your family

> CRUSH TIMIDITY AS IF IT WERE A FALSE IDOL, AND MAKE IT A HABIT TO COURAGEOUSLY OBEY GOD IN THE FACE OF FEAR.

and close friends. When we obey God and His scriptures, we build up our faith, which decreases timidity and helps us experience the spiritual boldness of God.

Here are new names we can take on in order to crush the lies of the enemy:

Old Name	New Name
Timid	Powerful, Loved, Disciplined *2 Timothy 1:7*
Weak	Strong *2 Corinthians 12:10*
Abandoned	Adopted *Romans 8:14-17*
Rejected	Chosen *1 Peter 2:4*
Defeated	Overcomer *1 John 5:4*
Unaccomplished	Impressive *Proverbs 22:29*
Incompetent	Able *Philippians 4:13*

Meditation Scriptures:

Proverbs 3:5-6- *Trust in the Lord with all your heart, and do not rely on your own understanding; in all your ways know Him, and He will make your paths straight.*

2 Corinthians 12:9-10- *But he said to me, My grace is sufficient for you, for my power is perfected in weakness. Therefore, I will most gladly boast all the more about my weaknesses, insults, hardships, persecutions, and in difficulties, for the sake of Christ. For when I am weak, then I am strong.*

I John 4:4- *You are from God, little children, and you have conquered them, because the One who is in you is greater than the one who is in the world.*

1 Thessalonians 2:13- *This is why we constantly thank God, because when you received the word of God that you heard from us, you welcomed it not as a human message, but as it truly is, the word of*

God, which also works effectively in you who believe.

Psalm 24:8- *Who is this King of glory? The LORD, strong and mighty, the LORD mighty in battle.*

Assuming A New Identity

1. When we build up our faith in the word of God, the voices that are not like His will get quieter. When we fill up our minds, our hearts, and our environment with the word of God, those voices that are not like His will get quieter. On which scripture will you meditate to make God's voice louder? You can use the old name/new name chart, or find your own scripture.

2. God called Gideon a *mighty warrior* before Gideon could see it himself. He needed Gideon to have a vision of how great he could be if he partnered with God. What do you envision yourself doing with the power of God backing you?

3. Gideon heard what the angel said and responded with questions. Even though he had doubt, he didn't say, 'No God, I won't go." He asked questions, but repeatedly received God's words as the higher authority over his questions and doubts. This points to our prayer life and our communication with God. Write a prayer to God about something you feel led to do but are afraid of doing. Ask God for courage and strength to do it.

three
elijah's situational timidity

THE PROPHET ELIJAH was as bold and as powerful as a lion. Surely, he was known to be anything but timid. So why mention Elijah in a book about timidity? Why mention this fearless man who challenged evil kings and false gods, and raised the dead?

1 Kings 17-19 recounts the reign of King Ahab and Queen Jezebel, when the Israelites were seduced by idol worship. The false gods, Baal and Asherah, were back on the scene, and people worshipped these gods in hopes that dew and rain would multiply their crops. Queen Jezebel nurtured efforts to bring these false gods into prominence. There were 450 prophets of Baal and

400 prophets of Asherah, and Jezebel ordered the deaths of all prophets of the true and living God. She wanted none of them alive and tried to make the Israelites forget their God forever.

God sent the prophet Elijah to tell King Ahab that no dew nor rain would fall on the land for years, unless he said so, because of their idolatry. Because this word was unpopular, and because Jezebel ordered all prophets of God to be killed, God sent Elijah out of town to retreat to safety and be nourished. On his retreat, Elijah experienced many miracles. The first miracle was God sending a raven to feed him as he journeyed on the road.

The second miracle happened when a widow and her son invited Elijah to stay in their house. The widow had enough water to share but not enough food. Elijah multiplied the widow's resources so she had enough to feed everyone for a few days. Then, when the widow's son became sick and died, Elijah brought the boy back to life. After this time of seeing God's miracles, Elijah was sent back to King Ahab to deliver the word that it was time to choose sides, that is, to prove who was the true and living God.

When the prophets of Baal offered up a slaughtered bull as a sacrifice, Baal did not respond. These prophets called on their god from morning to afternoon. Elijah made fun of them by asking if Baal was sleeping or had gone on vacation. When it was Elijah's turn to call on the one true God, God responded with fire that consumed the offering, the wood, the stones, and the dust.

Immediately, the people fell on their faces in worship. It was now unquestionable who the true and living God was. Elijah announced that God would send rain to bless the crops and end the drought, and He did. That day, God showed that He—

not the false idols—was the only source of blessings and fertile land. But, all of this made Jezebel furious and she threatened Elijah by saying he would be dead by the next day. She had already been successful in persecuting many of God's prophets, although some managed to escape Jezebel's wrath. It was recorded in 1 Kings 18:4 and v.13 that the prophet Obadiah had successfully hid 100 prophets. Still, Elijah felt his life was in danger. He was intimidated by Jezebel's words and ran for his life.

Elijah ran so long on an empty stomach and with nothing to drink, that he became exhausted and prayed for death until he fell asleep. How could Elijah be afraid of anyone or anything when he witnessed God perform all of those powerful miracles through him? Where did Elijah's boldness and faith go?

Ministry can be strenuous. The work God calls us to do can lead even the strongest to situations of fear and timidity. This timidity may show up in settings where you don't feel free to be yourself or act as you normally do. That is why we must live a life that sustains our calling. Elijah was called to bring truth to sinful, unwelcoming places. He had to face his enemies, live in unfamiliar places with people who worshipped false gods, and perform miracles. Imagine the spiritual warfare he went through, especially when he had to face King Ahab and Queen Jezebel, whose goal was to make their people turn away from the one true and living God.

When Elijah prayed for the dead boy to come alive again, and when he prayed for rain to fall, the Bible said he travailed and prayed laboriously (1 Kings 17, 18). A travail is likened to a woman giving birth; praying to move the hand of God on behalf of others is hard work!

If we really want to be free to live a life sustainable to our callings, we must choose between our own comfort and God's calling, but we can't have both. When we choose God's calling, we must also choose to develop *mind-body-spiritual care practices* that support that calling, and this includes a healthy lifestyle. If we don't live healthily and take care of our minds, bodies, and souls, we won't last very long in our callings and in ministry. It makes no sense to lead a life of doing God's work, only to have it cut short because of poor health and a lean soul (Mark 8:36-37).

> WHEN WE CHOOSE GOD'S CALLING, WE MUST ALSO CHOOSE TO DEVELOP MIND–BODY–SPIRITUAL CARE PRACTICES THAT SUPPORT THAT CALLING, AND THIS INCLUDES A HEALTHY LIFESTYLE.

Throughout Elijah's ordeal of running and eventually falling asleep, God restored him by providing food and keeping him safe. He ended up in the same location where his ancestor Moses, heard God's voice through the burning bush years ago (1 Kings 19:7-18). It was in this location, Mount Horeb, the mountain of God, that Elijah communed with God in his anxious state, and he spoke with God until he was centered and surrounded by peace. As Elijah retreated and spent time with God, God restored him and cared for his soul, so he would be strengthened and prepared for what was to come. God also sent Elijah someone to train. In this time with God, Elijah received instructions to train Elisha to be his successor. Elijah told God, that he had been zealous, felt alone, and was fearful that Jezebel would kill him like she had killed other prophets (1 Kings 19:10; again, we know from 1 Kings 18:4 that 100 of these true prophets were not dead but were safely in hiding). So, God told Elijah to begin training Elisha to take his place.

With God's help, and Elisha's companionship, Elijah was able to return to performing miracles and bringing truth to people in God's name. God performed soul care to Elijah so that he could overcome intimidation and get back to doing what he was called to do.

What does soul care look like? It looks like adequate rest (Matthew 11:28-30), exercise (1 Corinthians 9:27), healthy eating (Daniel 1:8, 15), fasting (Mark 9:29 NKJV), wise counsel (Proverbs 11:14), community (Proverbs 11:25), and reading and meditating on the word of God (John 6:35). All of these things are holy and help to replenish an exhausted soul. When we discipline our bodies to rest, and when we pray and read God's word to renew our minds and protect our souls, we experience more confidence and less timidity. Communing with

> WHEN WE DISCIPLINE OUR BODIES TO REST, AND WHEN WE PRAY AND READ GOD'S WORD TO RENEW OUR MINDS AND PROTECT OUR SOULS, WE EXPERIENCE MORE CONFIDENCE AND LESS TIMIDITY.

wise counsel, which can translate to counseling and therapy, is important for restoration. Discipleship and refreshing others with the knowledge we have contributes to our own vibrancy.

So, all of this means that resting, praying, reading God's word, healthy eating and exercise, wise counsel, and mentoring and building community with others, should be included in our *mind-body-spiritual care practices.* All of these things are holy and are necessary for overcoming timidity, moving courageously, and sustaining our callings. God meets us in our resting and retreating.

When the Bible says that we should present our bodies as living sacrifices, holy and acceptable unto God, which is our reasonable service, it is to state that being healthy and holy is not a suggestion. Being healthy is our service unto the Lord.

It is what we are expected to do. The Bible also says that we should beat our bodies to subjection so that we would not be disqualified from this fight. Let us not allow health issues to stand in the way of fulfilling God's plan for our lives. When we are our best selves, we can do more for God. When we lead healthy lives, we can be the bold, *unprideful light* God has called us to be.

Meditation Scriptures:

Mark 8:36-37- *What good is it for someone to gain the whole world, yet forfeit their soul? Or what can anyone give in exchange for their soul?*

Matthew 11:28-29- *Come to Me, all you who are weary and burdened, and I will give you rest. Take My yoke upon you and learn from Me, for I am gentle and humble in heart, and you will find rest for your souls.*

1 Peter 5:7- *Cast all your anxiety on Him because He cares for you.*

Romans 12:1- *Therefore, I urge you, brothers and sisters in view of God's mercy, to offer your bodies as a living sacrifice, holy and pleasing to God—this is your true and proper worship.*

John 6:35- *Then Jesus declared, "I am the Bread of life. Whoever comes to Me will never go hungry, and whoever believes in Me will never be thirsty."*

3 John 1:2- *Dear friend, I pray that you may enjoy good health and that all may go well with you, even as your soul is getting along well.*

Situational Timidity

1. Where or when do you feel most timid?

2. What is your plan to improve your health spiritually, mentally, and physically?

3. Fasting is not only turning away food. It is simply sacrificing or giving up something temporarily, and replacing it with praying and reading God's word. What can you periodically give up to replace with time with God? *(Examples are sweets, social media, television, caffeine, etc.; please consult your physician before fasting from food).*

four
jonah's reluctance and superiority

GOD'S STORY IS FIXED. His characters and the roles they play are up to His people. When I think of the book of Jonah, I think of the story of God's plan to save and redeem His people. God wanted Jonah to warn Nineveh, a city of sinners, that they had forty days to repent, or their city would be destroyed. But Jonah felt intimidated by the role he was given. He felt intimidated because he knew this city was powerful and could very well harm him if they didn't like what he said.

Jonah was a man of God who heard directly from God, but when God gave Him an order he didn't like, he ran. He didn't respond with consent nor questions. He just ran. And because he ran, he brought unnecessary trials upon himself. Believers have been known to ask God, "*Why*?", but they should *never* stop communicating with God. Cutting off communication with God is dangerous.

Jonah was instructed by God to go east to Nineveh, the capital of Assyria, but instead he booked a ride headed west to Tarshish. Because Jonah was on the ship to Tarshish when he should have been in transit to Nineveh, God caused wind to stir so strongly that it nearly ripped the ship apart.

CUTTING OFF COMMUNICATION WITH GOD IS DANGEROUS.

On the way to Tarshish, Jonah was comfortably sleeping. But the sailors around him, who were men of a different faith, were alarmed by the storms and figured out he was the cause of them. Jonah's disobedience to God not only put himself in danger, but it also risked the safety of the others on the ship.

These sailors woke Jonah up and made him face his disobedience. They asked him who he was and what his purpose was on the ship. Jonah was forced to tell the truth about his identity and the quest he was escaping. Even then, Jonah told the sailors to throw him off the boat. He would rather die than go to Nineveh, where God had told him to go. He was willing to sacrifice his life so **OBEYING GOD IS BETTER THAN SACRIFICING ANYTHING (1 SAMUEL 15:22). OBEDIENCE TO GOD IS MORE HONORABLE THAN OUR BENEVOLENCE.** those sailors would survive the storm, but he refused to go to Nineveh, where he could save thousands. Obeying God is better than sacrificing anything (1 Samuel 15:22). Obedience to God is more honorable than our benevolence.

The sailors were reluctant to throw Jonah over the boat, but they didn't know how else to stop the turbulence, so they did it. The storm calmed. These men weren't even believers of the same faith, but they asked Jonah's God for forgiveness for throwing him off the boat to his death.

Though Jonah was thrown into the sea, he didn't get the death he wanted. Who gets what they want when they run away from God? Jonah was swallowed by a big fish and was trapped inside its belly for three days.

Again, Jonah was forced to face his disobedience. In the belly of the whale, he prayed for God to save him. He gave God a psalm of surrender: "I will fulfill what I have vowed. Salvation belongs to the Lord" *(Jonah 2:9, Psalm 3:8)*. And with that, God caused the fish to spit Jonah out; God saved Jonah and gave him a second chance to do His will.

Finally, Jonah went to the city of Nineveh and spoke what the Lord told him to speak. The people actually listened and obeyed. As a matter of fact, they went above and beyond in receiving Jonah's message. They not only repented, but they clothed themselves with sackcloth and fasted. Every person on every level, from subjects to royals, repented, and God lifted their death sentences.

But Jonah was unforgiving. He was upset that the Ninevites met the forty-day window to be saved. He was upset that they turned from their wicked ways and repented. Jonah felt like they deserved to die for their wickedness. He didn't think they were worthy of receiving God's grace. That quickly, Jonah had forgotten how God rescued him from the fish's stomach. That quickly, he forgot that he himself was a beneficiary of God's redemption and grace.

Perhaps Jonah's story is one of the clearest to show how timidity is connected to pride:

- Jonah showed timidity by trying to run away from God. We can ask Jonah, *Who are you to break a vow and run away from what God has called you to do? (Numbers 30:2)*

- Jonah showed superiority by getting angry at the Ninevites for heeding his message and repenting for their sins. We can ask Jonah, *Who are you to think you can access God's grace but the Ninevites cannot?*

- Both in timidity and in superiority, Jonah showed that he was full of his own self-righteousness; he was not focused on the will of God.

One glaring problem of Jonah's is that he judged a sinful city — one that God described in Jonah 4:11 as a city of people who were not able to "tell their right hand from their left," — but Jonah didn't judge his own sin of denying what God told him to do...and Jonah *knew* his right from left when it came to obeying God!

The Bible says that we are to rejoice when a sinner repents (Luke 15:10, 32). Jonah did not rejoice when the Ninevites turned to God, but instead he maintained that they were not worthy to receive God's mercy. He sheltered himself just outside the city of Nineveh to look at them from afar, perhaps hoping they'd fall in sin again (Jonah 4:5). God had to show Jonah that while his focus was on how awful the Ninevites behaved, his focus needed to shift to how powerful God was to save an entire city from their sin. Look how easily Jonah's reluctance and timidity had shaped itself to pride. Jonah was able to proudly pray with psalms and restore his own position with God, but he failed to realize that God loved the Ninevites enough to save them, too.

> GOD HAD TO SHOW JONAH THAT WHILE HIS FOCUS WAS ON HOW AWFUL THE NINEVITES BEHAVED, HIS FOCUS NEEDED TO SHIFT TO HOW POWERFUL GOD WAS TO SAVE AN ENTIRE CITY FROM THEIR SIN.

In our own righteousness, we can feel so timid to speak out against mighty people. We can also be judgmental against them, and think that powerful sinners are not worthy of God's goodness.

This is where love is needed. Once we turn away from fear and timidity, it is so important for us to choose God's love. God's love — which involves loving Him above all else, and loving others as much as we love ourselves — will help us to gain a sound mind to remember that His core mission is to redeem the world and save His people from sin. God doesn't desire for anyone to perish or live in sin, and if we want to banish our timidity,

IN OUR OWN RIGHTEOUSNESS, WE CAN FEEL SO TIMID TO SPEAK OUT AGAINST MIGHTY PEOPLE. WE CAN ALSO BE JUDGMENTAL AGAINST THEM, AND THINK THAT POWERFUL SINNERS ARE NOT WORTHY OF GOD'S GOODNESS.

we must reflect this same passion in our hearts.

In loving God and ourselves, we must love others enough to pray that they turn away from their sin. We are to pray for their repentance. And when they accept Jesus, we are to rejoice; this is the *unprideful light* we must carry inside of us.

We don't know the fate of Jonah, but what we can learn from him, is how important it is to decide our role in God's story. Someone else's boldness caused you to be who you are today, so you ought to reciprocate non-reluctantly — you ought to never hold back what God has placed in you to share.

God's call should be perceived as a requirement, not a choice. That should be our perspective and how we demonstrate our love for Him (John 14:15). We need to know our role in God's story and play it with all of our being (Proverbs 16:1-5, 9). We need to pursue what He says, and not what is safe.

Meditation Scriptures:

Numbers 30:2- *When a man makes a vow to the Lord or takes an oath to obligate himself by a pledge, he must not break His word but must do everything he said.*

1 Samuel 15:22-23- *But Samuel replied: "Does the Lord delight in burnt offerings and sacrifices as much as in obeying the Lord? To obey is better than sacrifice, and to heed is better than the fat of rams. For rebellion is like the sin of divination, and arrogance like the evil of idolatry. Because you have rejected the word of the Lord, He has rejected you as king."*

Luke 15:10- *In the same way, I tell you, there is rejoicing in the presence of the angels of God over one sinner who repents.*

John 14:15- *If you love me, keep my commands.*

Proverbs 16:1-5- *To humans belong the plans of the heart, but from the LORD* *comes the proper answer of the tongue. All a person's ways seem pure to them, but motives are weighed by the LORD. Commit to the LORD whatever you do, and he will establish your plans. The LORD works out everything to its proper end—even the wicked for a day of disaster. The LORD detests all the proud of heart. Be sure of this: They will not go unpunished.*

Proverbs 16:9- *In their hearts humans plan their course, but the LORD establishes their steps.*

Psalm 3:8- *From the Lord comes deliverance. May Your blessing be on Your people.*

Jonah 2- *From inside the fish Jonah prayed to the Lord his God. He said: "In my distress, I called to the Lord, and He answered me. From deep in the realm of the dead, I called for help, and You listened to my cry. You hurled me into the depths, into the very heart of the seas, and the currents swirled around me; all Your waves and breakers swept over me. I said, 'I have been banished from Your* *sight; yet I will look again toward Your holy temple.' The engulfing waters threatened me, the deep surrounded me; seaweed was wrapped around my head. To the roots of the mountains I sank down; the earth beneath barred me in forever. But you, Lord my God, brought my life up from the pit. When my life was ebbing away, I remembered You, Lord, and my prayer rose to You, to Your holy temple. Those who cling to worthless idols turn away from God's love for them. But I, with shouts of grateful praise, will sacrifice to You. What I have vowed I will make good. I will say, 'Salvation comes from the Lord.'" And the Lord commanded the fish, and it vomited Jonah onto dry land.*

Trapped in Fish Guts

1. Recall a time when God told you to do something and you either refused to do it or were hesitant in doing it. What was the reason?

2. Take time to pray for any opportunities you have missed to carry out God's message of love and hope. Pray that these people have another chance to learn their *right hand from their left.*

Dear Lord, we thank you for your loving grace. We thank you for knowing the end from the beginning. We ask for forgiveness for not showing up to play our roles in your story, which is the story of love and salvation for the fallen world. Right now, we pray that You would create in us a clean heart that reflects Your love and mercy for Your people, remembering your love and mercy for us when we don't deserve it.

God, just as Jonah was able to call on You in his disobedience, we call on You to forgive us for being reluctant to carry out Your work.

Romans 8:1 says that God does not condemn us when we are in Him and when we walk after the Spirit and not the flesh—that is when we walk in obedience to Him. We thank You that we are free from condemnation from past mistakes. We recommit our vow to You to carry out Your work, and we pledge to carry Jesus, the Light of the world in us and will offer your love to others. We are so careful to remember that no one can earn Your goodness, and that is why You had to give up Your life. We know that salvation belongs to You, and You offer it freely to all who receive Your love and forgiveness. We pray for Your providential care, which has the power to create additional opportunities for people to hear the truth and learn their right from wrong. We thank You again for Your goodness, and for second chances.

*We renew our vow to be obedient to You,
to be quick to hear and swift to move
when You tell us to. Our inheritance is to
see Your word be fulfilled here on earth
as it is in heaven.*

In Jesus' name. AMEN.
******

five

woman with the issue of fear

W E HAVE EXPLORED a few men of the Old Testament, so now, let's spotlight a woman of the New Testament. This woman had an issue of blood, and the Bible said her faith made her whole. We know that faith is believing in the Lord, but there is also an active component to faith. Our faith should compel us to act or do something.

Mark 5:21-43 tells us that Jesus was called on by a church ruler named Jairus to raise his daughter from the dead. Jesus pushed through the crowd to heal Jairus' daughter, but his journey was interrupted when a woman who was ill appeared and touched his robe. This woman recognized the power of God on Jesus.

Perhaps she recognized that Jesus *was* God. Her faith compelled her to move, and when she touched Jesus' robe, she experienced instant healing. No one but Jesus noticed that someone had touched his robe. He stopped his travel to give this woman the opportunity to identify herself.

This woman had been living like a hermit, staying inside and remaining insecure about her position and standing in society. After twelve years of visiting doctors that could not treat her ailment, she ceased participating in everyday life outside of her home, because society had rejected her. But when Jesus visited her town, she had a decision to make. She left her house. I imagine her thoughts were, *This may be my last chance to receive my healing!* I'm sure it was a tough pursuit to get close to Jesus. The crowds surrounded Him, and she had to press through a lot of resistance to get to her healing.

When this woman reached her healing, she was not acknowledged. She must have felt many emotions being overlooked in a crowd that would condemn her if they noticed her; but in that moment, she was determined to break out of her timidity and get what she needed from the Lord. No one but the most powerful Healer Jesus noticed her. He asked the person who touched Him to identify herself.

Once hidden and shunned, the woman was now given the opportunity to testify in the open. Trembling with fear, this woman still demonstrated faith

> TREMBLING WITH FEAR, THIS WOMAN STILL DEMONSTRATED FAITH BY STEPPING FORWARD TO SPEAK TRUTH ABOUT HER TOUCHING JESUS' ROBE AND RECEIVING HER HEALING (MARK 5:33).

by stepping forward to speak truth about her touching Jesus' robe and receiving her healing (Mark 5:33).

Then, Jesus said, "Your faith has made you whole" (Mark 5:34). Jesus was able to stop and acknowledge this courageous woman, and he still made time to heal the church ruler's daughter too.

This woman with the issue of fear is not named in the Bible, but you can view this as an opportunity to insert your name and remember that no matter how small, unimportant, fearful, or ashamed you may feel, God sees you, knows you, and He says you belong to Him. To Jesus, it does not matter if you are a ruler or follower, or if your upbringing or previous experiences were favorable or unfortunate. God still claims you and calls you His own. He has called you to be full and overflowing with His powerful light that shines brightly for Him. May you be hidden no more. Even if your voice shakes because of fear, speak truth and shine brightly for God!

We who have issues with timidity need to understand that power comes after *finally* deciding to do what the Lord has told us to do. This seemingly insignificant woman was significant and powerful enough to appear in our Bible. God knew that we needed to learn her story in order to model her courageous faith that compelled her to move. We must understand how powerful it is to decide that we will take God at His word, and we will make contact with Him. We must see the power in stating that we will do what He says and adopt His will for our lives. When we do that, we are exercising our faith, and only good can come out of that.

> WE MUST SEE THE POWER IN STATING THAT WE WILL DO WHAT HE SAYS AND ADOPT HIS WILL FOR OUR LIVES.

Whatever it is that you feel God is telling you to do, He would never tell you to shrink back. God is always calling you to be bold and confident in Him. God is calling you to act on *something.* He wants you to exercise your faith, to further the kingdom of God, and to speak truth.

> GOD IS ALWAYS CALLING YOU TO BE BOLD AND CONFIDENT IN HIM. GOD IS CALLING YOU TO ACT ON SOMETHING.

So, what is it that you have to share with the kingdom? How can you work to bring forth His glory? It is not enough that we receive the Lord. Receiving the Lord is awesome. To live a purposeful life that advances God's kingdom is the calling of a Christian. Receiving God is our salvation, and devoting our lives to furthering His kingdom is His calling for us. So today, will you answer the call? Not only are you in the company of people surrounding you, but you are also in the company of people in the Bible.

You should now feel a greater assurance that God will be with you and will meet you in every circumstance when you call out to Him.

RECEIVING GOD IS OUR SALVATION, AND DEVOTING OUR LIVES TO FURTHERING HIS KINGDOM IS HIS CALLING FOR US.

Matthew 5:16- Let your light shine before others, that they may see your good deeds and glory your Father in heaven.

We have a light and it is shining. We cannot hide it. It is not His will for us to hide it. It *is* His will for us to make a mark on this world. Let's make a mark on this world for Jesus.

Meditation Scriptures:

Matthew 5:16- *In the same way, let your light shine before others, that they may see your good deeds and glorify your Father in heaven.*

Mark 5:33- *Then the woman, knowing what had happened to her, came and fell at His feet and, trembling with fear, told Him the whole truth.*

Philippians 2:12-13- *Therefore my dear friends, as you have always obeyed—not only in my presence, but now much more in my absence—continue to work out your salvation with fear and trembling, 13 for it is God who works in you to will and to act in order to fulfill his good purpose.*

Speak Truth, Even If Your Voice Shakes. *~Maggie Kuhn*

1. Recall a time when you demonstrated courage in the face of fear.

six
timothy receives the torch

W HEN BELIEVERS OF God disciple and mentor the next generation, great things happen. This is the story of Timothy, who came from a natural and spiritual family of believers. Timothy's Jewish mother, Eunice, and grandmother, Lois, passed on to him the tradition of following Christ. As a young man, Timothy also received instruction to follow Christ from his mentor and spiritual father, Paul. Not much is mentioned about his natural father, who was Greek (Acts 16:1).

First and Second Timothy are letters Paul wrote to encourage Timothy to assist the Ephesus church in his absence, and to be bold at a time when spreading the gospel of Jesus Christ was dangerous (2 Timothy 4:5).

At the time of writing the first letter, Paul was in Macedonia, and by the time he wrote the second letter, he was imprisoned in Rome and awaiting execution. In a sense, Paul was transferring courage to Timothy, and reminding him how noble it was to stand up for the gospel of Jesus. Paul knew what it was like to be persecuted and imprisoned for his faith, and because he was a former killer of Christians prior to converting to Christianity, he also knew that he owed Christ his life. Paul was a warrior, who humbly gave his life to the cause of spreading the gospel of Jesus. He was a perfect example of courage to Timothy.

There were many problems in the Ephesus church, and Paul gave Timothy guidance on how to solve these problems.

In the first letter, Paul urged Timothy to teach people how to preach sound doctrine, which pointed to the love and gospel of Jesus Christ, rather than legalism and inaccurate teachings. He also modeled to

PAUL WAS A WARRIOR, WHO HUMBLY GAVE HIS LIFE TO THE CAUSE OF SPREADING THE GOSPEL OF JESUS. HE WAS A PERFECT EXAMPLE OF COURAGE TO TIMOTHY.

Timothy empathetic leadership by showing how he identified as the chief of sinners, which allowed him to be a more loving, non-judgmental example to others (1 Timothy 1:16).

Then, Paul tells Timothy to hold regular prayer meetings and pray for everyone, including those in authority, and to lead with the idea that God desires all to be saved.

It must have been very intimidating to take over an entire church in Paul's absence, but

Timothy had to do it. There were men and women of all ages in his church, and he had to preach to them all.

Timothy had to give specific instruction to men and women who were distracting each other from God. He had to correct men who were debating doctrine during worship, and he had to correct women who dressed in flashy attire as if they were attending a fashion show. This was important, because members needed to be focused on God, rather than viewing each other as better or worse off, or as more or less knowledgeable (1 Timothy 2:8-10, 6:17-19).

> IT MUST HAVE BEEN VERY INTIMIDATING TO TAKE OVER AN ENTIRE CHURCH IN PAUL'S ABSENCE, BUT TIMOTHY HAD TO DO IT.

Paul also gave Timothy guidelines on the types of people to appoint as leaders and deacons. At this particular church, there seemed to be a practice of women usurping authority from men, instead of working collaboratively. For this reason, Paul told Timothy to ban women from teaching men, and he did not specify if or when this ban would be lifted. However, this does not mean that Paul did not approve of women leading in the church. It must be noted that in other letters, Paul affirmed courageous women leaders, such as:

- Priscilla, along with her husband, Aquila, who hosted the church in their home, and taught a preacher how to better explain the gospel of Jesus. *(Acts 18:24-26; Romans 16:3-5).*

- Deacon Phoebe of the church in Cenchreae, who supported the cause of spreading the gospel. *(Romans 16:1-2).*

- Mary, a hard worker and servant-leader *(Romans 16:6).*

- Junia who was imprisoned with Paul, and was among the apostles, which indicates that either she was an apostle or highly esteemed by the apostles of her day *(Romans 16:7).*

Also in Paul's letters were instructions on how to correct elders versus how to correct young people. Elders were to be exhorted as parents, and young people were to be corrected as siblings. Timothy had times of feeling timid, but Paul told him not to fear and not to let anyone despise him for being young and teaching the gospel (1 Timothy 4:12).

TIMOTHY HAD TIMES OF FEELING TIMID, BUT PAUL TOLD HIM NOT TO FEAR AND NOT TO LET ANYONE DESPISE HIM FOR BEING YOUNG AND TEACHING THE GOSPEL (I TIMOTHY 4:12).

In his letter, Paul warned Timothy that some would leave the church after being influenced by the world. He warned Timothy to not give up, even when others would. He told him to continue teaching sound doctrine and to continue "fighting the good fight of faith" (1 Timothy 6:12).

In 1 Timothy 4:11-14, Paul reassured Timothy that he had a God-given gift to speak and build up the church, and he reminded him that his gift was prayed over and nurtured by his mother, grandmother, and Paul himself (2 Timothy 1:5; 3:14-15).

Paul instructed Timothy to be an example in speech and conduct, and to publicly read and teach the gospel of Jesus Christ for the spiritual nourishment of the church, and for his own spiritual care. He told him, "Pay close attention to your life and your teaching; persevere in these things, for in doing this you will save yourself and your hearers" (1 Timothy

4:16).

Paul also wrote to Timothy about how to care for widows and elders. He told him how to empower people from all stations of life, from the poor to the wealthy. He instructed the wealthy not to flaunt their possessions, but to instead, use their wealth for good. He closed the letter with the same warning in his opening, which was to continue preaching sound doctrine, and to stop anyone from preaching doctrine that confused the hearers.

Paul's second letter was a more intense call for young Timothy to be courageous. Paul realized that his death was approaching (2 Timothy 4:6, 18). He took one last chance to remind Timothy that the spirit of God inside of him was greater than his timidity. He was called to stand up for Christ in the midst of his timidity. Paul took time to remind Timothy of his Christian heritage Essentially, Paul told Timothy:

Remember who you are and where you come from. You are the son of Eunice and the grandson of Lois. You have my mantle of leadership, and the spirit of God is in you. I laid my own hands on you and prayed for you. You are called by God and are empowered by the Spirit of God to do this work. You can do this. You can help this church. "Therefore, I remind you to rekindle the gift of God that is in you through the laying on of my hands, for God has not given you a spirit of fear, but one of power, love, and sound judgment" (2 Timothy 1:6).

Paul showed Timothy how to combat his timidity by telling him to remember who he was and to know that he had power, love, and a sound mind:

- Power from the Holy Spirit to steer the church in the right direction

- Love and empathy for the body of Christ

- A sound mind to make good decisions, and to hold fast to correct doctrine in Paul's absence

Then, Paul reminded Timothy that he was once in his place. It took radical courage for Timothy to remain faithful to Christ in such dangerous times, and in the absence of his mentor Paul. In following Paul's instructions, Timothy learned to be unashamed of the gospel of Jesus Christ; Timothy was able to do this successfully by none other than the

Holy Spirit who empowered him and gave him grace to stand in the absence of Paul:

2 Timothy 1:14- *Guard the good deposit through the Holy Spirit who lives in us.*

Unpridefully Receive The Torch And Light It For Jesus

Not all Christians are pastors or church leaders, but all Christians are called to tell others around them about Jesus Christ (Matthew 5:16, Mark 16:15). Like Timothy, we may feel uncomfortable to do what God has called us to do, but we must follow Paul's example in unashamedly and unpridefully shining our lights for Jesus Christ. Shining your light for Jesus looks like humbly serving Christ by pursuing your calling and going where God sends you. Timidity may creep in to tell you that you are

SHINING YOUR LIGHT FOR JESUS LOOKS LIKE HUMBLY SERVING CHRIST BY PURSUING YOUR CALLING AND GOING WHERE GOD SENDS YOU.

unqualified to work for God, due to a range of reasons. Maybe you lack knowledge of the word; that can be remedied by becoming a student of the word and attending Bible studies and life groups. Perhaps you feel you lack a Christian heritage. Believers should never feel like they are without family; the heritage of a believer is the body of Christ, which is the family of God.

Every believer's mantle is to be an empathetic, *unprideful light* that draws people to Christ. Our goal is to live abundantly, and to pursue greater works than seen in the days of Jesus, by way of His Spirit, which lives inside of us *(John 14:12-26; 1 John 4:4).*

Paul did not start life well. He started out persecuting Christians, but once he came to his senses, he gave Christ his all. And so, Paul pressed Timothy to give his all and to not let timidity stop him from fulfilling his calling. For Timothy, to listen would be wise, and to not listen would be prideful.

So, what does that mean for you? You have been passed the baton; it is up to you. The late Christian leader Myles Munroe stated, "Don't die old, die empty. That's the goal of life. Go to the cemetery and disappoint the graveyard." In other words, spend your time productively on this earth, giving your all to God.

Reflecting on Your Christian Heritage

1. Below, make a list of warriors for Christ from your family, local church, or the media whom you admire. State how you've been empowered by them.

2. *Complete and recite this affirmation:*

    (Your name) _____,
    remember who you are. You come
    from _____

    _____

    _____,

    and the spirit of God is in you.
    You are called by God and are
    empowered by the Spirit of God to
    do this work. You can do this.
    "Therefore, I remind you to
    rekindle the gift of God that is in
    you through the laying on of my
    hands, for God has not given you
    a spirit of fear, but one of power,
    love, and sound judgment" (2
    Timothy 1:6).

seven
dethrone timidity

I N THE INTRODUCTORY chapter, we defined pride as "choosing to believe one's own thoughts and follow one's own will over God's thoughts and God's will." We know that for a moment, Moses chose to believe that he could not liberate his people, even when God told him he would. We know that for a moment, Gideon chose to believe that he was not a mighty warrior, even when God told him he was. We know that for a moment, Elijah believed he would be killed for exposing false gods. We know that Jonah thought he would be killed for telling an entire city to repent from their evil ways. We know that the woman with the issue of fear thought she would be overlooked by Jesus, but she was noticed by Him and was given space to speak truth even when her voice trembled. And we know that Timothy thought he was too young to lead a church, but he was called by God to do just that.

I once thought I was unable to create. I belong to a creative family. My husband and I met while creating music. Our daughter, who is biologically his from a previous marriage, is a thespian. We create all of the time. But early in our union, I faced a traumatic experience and consequently chose to believe a lie over God's truth.

I was pregnant once, but nine weeks in, I miscarried. I was unable to get pregnant again. The doctor used the term *unexplained infertility* when giving the diagnosis.

This term was foreign to me, because, in my mind, I was a person who created all of the time. When we learned that there would be difficulties in creating a child and adding to our family, I became timid and uncertain in all areas of my life. I focused on my inabilities and found it challenging to create music, prose, *anything.* I started to believe the lie that I was unable to create anything at all. I knew the truth, that God was sovereign and His strength could be made perfect in my weakness. But, at the time, I did

> I KNEW THE TRUTH, THAT GOD WAS SOVEREIGN AND HIS STRENGTH COULD BE MADE PERFECT IN MY WEAKNESS. BUT AT THE TIME, I DID NOT GIVE GOD THE OPPORTUNITY TO SHOW HIS STRENGTH IN MY INFIRMITY.

not give God the opportunity to show His strength in my infirmity. I succumbed to my frailty, and I departed from the creative gifts He gave me. I paused my life.

I sought out community, but found it hard to locate safe spaces. Friends I once had didn't fully acknowledge my family as complete. I found fewer things in common with loved ones, and nowhere felt safe. Community is a must in hard seasons like this, but at the time, the only community I had exacerbated my pain.

Feeling lost, I searched for something concrete with meaning and immediate rewards. I began working very hard on tasks that didn't fulfill me, for a paycheck. I lost myself in busyness. I became so busy in many great things, but ignored what God told me to do, because I thought that God's will for me to create was no longer attainable.

Through this time, I earned a degree and started a career, but still I was unfulfilled. I never stopped praying for God to send me a trustworthy community of people who had experiences like mine, but who lived triumphantly, and eventually He did. I found women with similar stories, and for the first time, I saw that I was not alone. I felt like I could still find purpose in this life. This women's group (Chante Truscott and

Wives in Waiting) helped me recover from my trauma and find grace to live unpridefully for Jesus.

At first, I lived to help others succeed. I saw my abilities come alive in the work I did for others. There is nothing wrong with helping others, but I found that self-sacrificing for another person's dream leads to exhaustion. I was not prioritizing God's dream for my life. I neglected the life-giving work He had given me to do. I was using my abilities to help others reach their purpose and potential, while living short of mine.

One day during church service, my pastor at the time (Kenneth Mulkey) interrupted his sermon to say that he had a prophetic word for someone. I had never before seen him do this. The word from God was for a couple experiencing fertility issues. The congregation was huge; he didn't spotlight or call attention to anyone. He simply spoke the word over the pulpit. He recited the following scripture to the couple:

Isaiah 54:1- *Sing, O barren woman, you who never bore a child; burst into song, shout for joy, you who were never in labor; because more are the children of the desolate woman than of her who has a husband," says the LORD.*

Then, he resumed his sermon. But I was stuck on that scripture. It resonated with me, and I felt God telling me to *sing.* Live again. *Sing.* Worship God and live again.

> **FINALLY, I HAD TO RECOMMIT MYSELF TO GOD. I HAD TO COMMIT TO LIVING COURAGEOUSLY IN THE FACE OF FEAR.** IT WAS EASY TO HELP OTHERS, BUT TO HIDE MYSELF WHEN GOD TOLD ME TO SHINE HIS LIGHT WAS DISOBEDIENCE TO HIM. SO, I STARTED SHOWING UP IN LIFE.

So, finally, I had to recommit myself to God. I had to commit to living courageously in the face of fear. It was easy to help others, but to hide myself when God told me to shine His light was disobedience to Him. So, I started showing up for my life. I started singing again. I started writing. I started to create for God again. It felt inauthentic at first, but I was coming alive in my true self. I refused to succumb to the slow death and erasure of making my mark on the earth. I had to tell myself:

The season of hiding in timidity is over. Now is the time to press play on my life and allow God to work in me.

I was made to create. God ordained me to create. And finally, I started to push through timidity to create!

Today is the day to dethrone timidity and allow God to work freely in your life. Timidity, like conceit and all other prideful enemies of God, works to bind God's people and prevent us from becoming our

> LIVING FOR GOD IS NEVER ABOUT OUR ABILITIES OR LACK OF, BUT IT'S ABOUT WHAT HE WANTS TO DO IN US.

authentic selves. Timidity is a work of the flesh, and we must tell our flesh to bow to the will of God. We must tell our flesh to decrease so that God can increase in our lives, because living for God is never about our abilities or lack of, but it's about what *He* wants to do in us. It's God's show, and His light is in us. We must courageously shine our *Unprideful Light*.

Matthew 5:16- *In the same way, let your light shine before others, that they may see your good deeds and glorify your Father in heaven.*

Meditation Scriptures:

2 Chronicles 7:14- *If my people, who are called by my name, will humble themselves and pray and seek my face and turn from their wicked ways, then I will hear from heaven, and I will forgive their sin and will heal their land.*

I Peter 5:5-6- *God resists the proud, but gives grace to the humble.*

John 3:30- *He must become greater; I must become less.*

John 15:5- *I am the Vine; you are the branches. If you remain in Me and I in you, you will bear much fruit; apart from Me you can do nothing.*

Philippians 1:6- *being confident of this, that he who began a good work in you will carry it on to completion until the day of Christ Jesus.*

1 Corinthians 14:1- *Follow the way of love and eagerly desire gifts of the Spirit, especially prophecy.*

Isaiah 43:6-7- *I will say to the north, 'Give them up!' and to the south, 'Do not hold them back.' Bring my sons from afar and my daughters from the ends of the earth—**everyone who is called by my name, whom I created for my glory, whom I formed and made."***

Ephesians 2:10- *For we are God's handiwork, created in Christ Jesus to do good works, which God prepared in advance for us to do.*

Mark 9:24- *"...I do believe; help me overcome my unbelief!"*

Recommitment Prayer

Dear God, I admit that I have lost my way. Forgive me for disobeying you and not believing that You can perform Your will in me. Help me to find my way back to You, and to find my purpose in You. I humble myself and ask that You would help me become who You have created me to be. Help me live my days in service to You. Reveal to me Your dream for my life. Show me how to be Your light that draws men to You and brings You glory. I worship You. In Jesus' name, AMEN.

Wait for God to respond and record His dream for you here:

Chapter 7 References

1. Mulkey, K. (2017, March 9). A Study of Psalm 119 | Kenneth Mulkey Ep. 2.

2. Munroe, M. (2018, July 4). Die Empty.

Join the *Unprideful Light* Community on Facebook at:

www.chontalikirk.com

www.ingramcontent.com/pod-product-compliance
Lightning Source LLC
Chambersburg PA
CBHW071228090426
42736CB00014B/3012